Testaments in Stone

The Nonconformist Chapels
of
Bradford on Avon

James Holden

Bradford on Avon Museum

Published in 2024 by
Ex Libris Press
www.ex-librisbooks.co.uk

in association with
Bradford on Avon Museum
www.bradfordonavonmuseum.com

Origination by Ex Libris Press
Bradford on Avon

Cover design by Jenny Holden

Map by Karen Pigott

ISBN 9781912020027

Printed by CPI Ltd.
Chippenham, Wiltshire

This book has been generously supported by Bradford on Avon Quakers, Old Baptist Chapel and United Church, Bradford on Avon

Contents

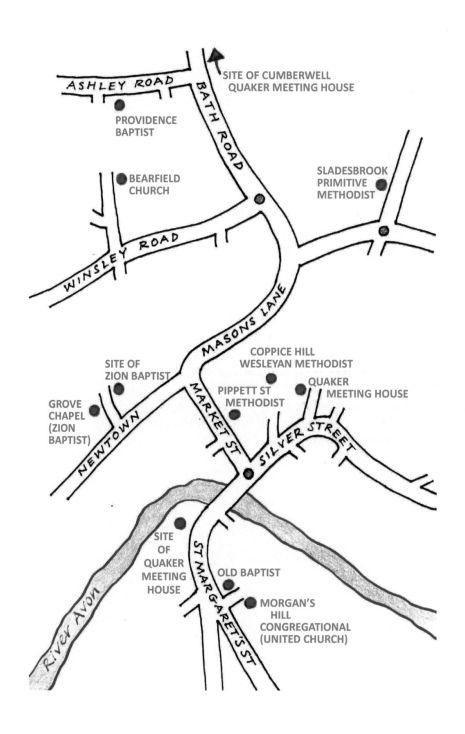

1 Introduction

The 17th century was a time of unprecedented religious upheaval in England. More and more people felt that the Protestant Reformation of the previous century had not gone far enough in removing what they saw as the corruption and oppressive ritual of the Catholic church. They wished to worship in a different, simpler and purer way, and formed a host of different small groups to do so. By mid-century these had coalesced into four main sects, the Presbyterians, Independents, Baptists and Quakers.

After the Civil War and the execution of Charles the First the puritans were in control, and this meant more freedom for these groups to worship as they chose. But when Charles the Second was restored to the throne in 1660 he immediately turned the clock back. Anyone who dissented from the teachings of the Church of England was persecuted: fined, locked up, sometimes beaten up and occasionally even killed. Only late in the century did the pressure ease, but even then discrimination was intense. It was well into the 19th century before the last barriers to nonconformists participating fully in society were removed.

Early nonconformist worship was hidden: they met in each other's houses, in barns and in the open air, ever fearful that their meetings would be disrupted. So when at last they had the confidence to build their own places of worship this was a hugely significant moment. The resulting chapels were built with the greatest care, testaments in stone to the faith of the congregation.

Bradford has a fine set of chapels, ranging in date from the end of the 17th century to the middle of the 19th. Both the buildings themselves and their histories are of interest, and in this book I have separated out these two aspects so that each can be described clearly. The first part tells the stories of how the different denominations became established in the town and the many changes which have occurred thereafter. The second part examines firstly the basic principles which determine chapel design and then the particular building history of each one. A final short chapter looks at a few of the individuals who have played an important part in the chapel story.

There is no shortage of interesting buildings in this town but the chapels, though not conspicuous, are amongst the most interesting of all. The nonconformists started as a small minority in troubled times but gradually grew in number until by the mid-19th century they were a majority amongst the townspeople. It is this combination of the buildings and the history being created within them which lends such fascination to the story of nonconformity in Bradford on Avon, and I hope this short guide will provide a useful introduction.

A note on terminology. Early nonconformists were usually called 'dissenters'. 'Nonconformist' came into general use later and by the late 19th century the term 'free church' was often used, implying that people attending such churches defined themselves as worshipping as they chose, not as refusing to meet some standard of normal behaviour. Early nonconformist buildings were generally called meeting houses, and Quaker buildings have been called this ever since; other denominations mainly used the name 'chapel' but the term 'church' also came into common use, generally for the body of people rather than specifically for the building.

Photographs accompanying the text are mine except where otherwise credited.

James Holden
Bradford on Avon
July 2024

2 The Nonconformist Story

The Struggle for Freedom –
Dissenting Religion in Bradford in the 17th Century

The Protestant Reformation in England, though it may have been started off by the requirements of Henry VIII's love-life, was more deeply rooted in the wish to escape what was seen as the corruption and offensive ritual of the Catholic church.[1] But in the eyes of many the Protestant settlement imposed by Queen Elizabeth did not go far enough: they wished to strip away church ceremony, formulaic prayers and 'idolatrous' ornament and instead seek God by reading the Bible, praying in groups and listening to the evangelical sermons of learned and zealous ministers.

By the start of the 17th century 'Puritan' views like these had been present for a hundred years and more, but this was the century in which they came to the fore, helped of course by their proponents being on the winning side in the Civil War. By the time of the Commonwealth period, up to 1660, they were very much in the ascendant, with many parish churches in the hands of Puritan ministers and other religious groups blossoming. Of these the Presbyterians, governed by representative assemblies of elders, came to the fore in the 1650s; Independents believed each congregation should be entirely self-governing, and almost all renamed themselves as Congregationalists in later years; Baptists, with their belief in the importance of adult baptism, were relatively late on the scene as were the Quakers, more correctly known as the Society of Friends, who believed in direct experience of Christ without the aid of clergy.

By 1660 Bradford had a Quaker meeting taking place at Cumberwell on the Bath road out of town, reportedly attracting congregations of 300 to 400.[2] There were certainly groups of Presbyterians in Bradford at that date as well, and probably also Baptists. But then came the Restoration: Charles the Second, who some might have thought would go easy on dissenting religion given what had happened to his father, acted swiftly to turn the clock back. A series of Acts of Parliament followed, all designed to make dissent from the practices of the Church of England as difficult as possible. These were motivated perhaps as much by the fear of dissenting religion destabilising the newly re-established monarchy as by objection to the dissenters' religious beliefs.

But people had had some freedom of worship during the Commonwealth period and were not going to give it up easily. They met in each other's houses, in barns, in fields, ever watchful for the forces of the Justices of the Peace who might assault them, break up their meetings and at the worst arrest and imprison them. The dissenters met in large numbers – a meeting of 200 Presbyterians at the house of John Crooke, a Bradford farmer, is mentioned in 1669 and there were said to be area-wide meetings of up to 2,000 Presbyterians nearby – and they increasingly resisted attempts to disrupt their meetings, using staves to beat off attackers and even threatening the use of firearms.[3]

King Charles issued a 'Declaration of Indulgence' in 1672, suspending penal statutes against nonconformists. A number of groups took advantage of this: John Holton, a Bradford clothier, had his house registered for Presbyterian worship, an early sign of the support of the town's clothiers which was to be of vital importance later.[4] The house of John Lydiard and the barn of John Broomejohn were similarly licensed for Baptist worship.[5] Henry Shrapnel of St Margaret's Street, also a Baptist, had his house licensed and it was his son Zachariah who later gave the land for the first Baptist chapel to be built (see below).[6]

The Declaration of Indulgence was unexpected and caused widespread opposition from those who thought it reflected the King's Catholic sympathies: he was forced to repeal it the following year. The rest of the 1670s and the early 1680s produced continuing repression of dissenters but did not dampen their enthusiasm. A census in 1679, initiated by the bishop, showed 159 dissenters in Bradford parish against 3,105 conformists, but this probably understated the numbers of the former, who were widely supported.[7]

It might be thought that to construct a meeting house during this period was looking for trouble but the Quakers did, albeit at Cumberwell so well outside the town and hence less likely to provoke attack.[8] The **Cumberwell Quaker Meeting House** is believed to have been built in 1676, then rebuilt before 1689.[9] The Quakers also had a burial ground there, in use for a hundred years.

The short reign of James the Second (1685-88) turned the focus of religious dispute onto the king's Catholicism and his efforts to promote this in the government of the country, resulting eventually in the 'Glorious Revolution' of 1688 in which he was forced off the throne and replaced by his daughter Mary and her Dutch husband William, both firmly Protestant. With the emphasis on combatting Catholicism some of the pressure was taken off the Protestant nonconformists even before 1688, and William and Mary acted swiftly to take this further, promoting the Act of Toleration in early 1689. This Act gave freedom of worship to nonconformists who had taken the oath of allegiance but not to Catholics nor to those who did not believe in the Holy Trinity (Unitarians). Nonconformist places of worship had to be registered and toleration did not extend to removing other restrictions such as refusing them attendance at the universities or banning them from holding political office.

This was a major change. Nonconformists were discriminated against, opposed and bullied for a further hundred years and more, but at least they could now worship legally. Bradford's Baptists had been meeting for some years before this date, perhaps associated with the Southwick church which was highly influential as an early centre for Particular Baptists.[10] An 'Anabaptist conventicle' was reported by the churchwardens in 1662[11] and Baptists had been worshipping at the house of Henry Shrapnel since 1672, almost certainly that at 6-7 St Margaret's Street (then one house, as it is again now) which still contains a room possibly designed for worship.[12] Now they were quick to act: they registered the house of the 'widow Miller' in 1689 and that same year built their first chapel off St Margaret's Street[13] on land given to them on a 1,000 year lease by Zachariah Shrapnel.[14] The Baptist Chapel, which stood until 1797, occupied much of the same site as its successor, now called the Old Baptist, but was accessed from St Margaret's Hill.

6-7 St Margaret's Street, probably an early meeting place for Baptists

The strength of the Presbyterians in these early years has already been mentioned and it is not surprising that the third and last meeting house built in the 17th century, and the only one still standing, was for this group. The Grove Meeting House, at the end of Middle Rank on the hillside north of the town centre, was built in about 1698 on land belonging to Anthony Methuen and conveyed in that year to Francis Yerbury and his son, also Francis.[15] Both families were clothiers, and the support of such prominent people helps to show why nonconformist religion became established so firmly and so quickly in Bradford. It is worth noting also that both Methuen and Francis Yerbury (presumably the elder) in this same period registered buildings belonging to them for religious worship.[16]

Nonconformity Established – the 18th Century

The 18th century brought little of the external political turmoil of the 17th, but there was plenty going on within the nonconformist churches. For centuries there had been just one form of religion permitted in England, but the upheavals of the last hundred years left people questioning the articles of faith in a way which had not seemed possible in the past, and this in its turn led to further splits.

In Bradford this started with the **Grove Meeting House**, initially highly successful with congregations of up to 400 in the 1720s, a large number for such a modest space although at that date it did have first-floor galleries on three sides.[17] It was attended by wealthy clothiers and the like including, it was said, two members of parliament and 'six or eight carriages at a time'.[18] But in the 1730s an associate pastor was suspended for expressing Unitarian views: a belief, at that time illegal, that only God is divine. It turned out, however, that much of the congregation held similar views and it was the minister, Dr Josiah Read, and those who thought like him who had to leave. It seems that the chapel then became more Unitarian and remained that way through into the following century, though from the 1780s onwards it was in steep decline.

Dr Read and his associates resolved to set up their own church as Independents and did so in 1739.[19] The leading lights alongside Dr Read, himself an old man by now, were John Pitman of Bradford and Walter Grant of Monkton Farleigh, and it seems that when they left the Grove meeting house they worshipped first at Pitman's house, which was registered for worship in January 1739.[20] By 1741 their chapel at Morgan's Hill (later renamed St Margaret's Hill) was built, on land given by Mary Grant, wife of Walter, and with the aid of donations of £100 each from Read, Walter Grant and Pitman. The **Morgan's Hill Chapel**, now the United Church,

Morgan's Hill Congregational, much altered since its erection in 1741

appears to have had a small congregation throughout the 18th century, although 'very respectable'.[21] But the congregation was large enough for them to feel the need to lengthen the building by 12ft in 1798. The trustees, whose generosity in funding the chapel was remarkable – Grant and Pitman also left property worth over £2,000 to the chapel in their wills – seem to have treated the minister as their servant, something which caused friction on several occasions.

The first half of the 18th century was generally a time of consolidation, with no great expansion of nonconformity but nevertheless many chapels being built to replace meetings in houses, barns and the like. All this changed around mid-century with the arrival of Methodism, the spark which lit a religious revival. The name was coined to describe the supposedly 'methodical' way of life of a group of Oxford academics in the 1730s, of whom John Wesley and his brother Charles were two. After 1738 John Wesley, their leading light, turned away from seeking his personal salvation through this disciplined way of living and instead sought to bring salvation to others through evangelical preaching. He toured the country, his powerful preaching drawing large crowds. Though he always considered himself an Anglican and would not preach at the same time as Anglican services, nevertheless his appeal was such that he was resented by the existing churches. He came to Bradford early in his career, in July 1739, and asked both the vicar of Holy Trinity and the minister of the Grove chapel for permission to preach in their churches, but he was refused and instead resorted to preaching on Bearfield where, he said, a thousand people came to hear him.[22] He came here again several times that year, not again for a further ten years, but then regularly right up to not long before his death in 1791.[23]

It is not clear whether there was any Methodist organisation in the town after Wesley's 1739 visits or whether the initial appeal of Methodism was just his preaching, those who went to hear him continuing to attend Holy Trinity for Sunday worship. Certainly no meeting place for Methodists seems to have been registered until 1756 when a new chapel on Pippett Street (now Market Street) was opened.[24] The **Pippett Street Methodist** was built by Richard Pearce on the site of a former malthouse behind the Maidenhead Inn, of which he was landlord.[25] The Maidenhead Inn, after various different uses, had become by 2024 the Stumble Inn.

The motivation to build may well have been so that Wesley's meetings could be held there, and it was strongly associated with him: a clock he was said to have preached in front of is still in the building. Bradford soon became the head of Methodism in

John Wesley is said to have preached in front of this clock at Pippett Street Methodist

11

north Wiltshire and it remained the centre of a circuit of itinerant preachers until well into the 19th century.

The vigour of the newly established Methodists spilled over and encouraged growth in both the Independents (later Congregationalists) and Baptists. Indeed when the vicar of the parish church came to make his report to the Bishop in response to the 'Visitation Queries' of 1783, he replied to a question on nonconformists by saying that they were present 'of almost every denomination under Heaven innumerable. There are also two Methodist meetings supplied by a variety of teachers.'[26]

The Baptists thrived to the extent that they were able to rebuild their much-dilapidated chapel at the century's end in 1797.[27] The original had been accessed by an alley alongside but they were now able to buy the buildings in front and cut an archway through to the new and much larger chapel, an access which remains to this day.

But the same positive picture was not true for the Presbyterians and the Quakers. The Presbyterians at the Grove Meeting House, now Unitarian, went into steep decline towards the century's end, a common trend for Presbyterian meeting houses across England. The Quakers, no longer needing to be so hidden, in 1718 built a new meeting house in the town centre, off St Margaret's Street in what is now the car park outside St Margaret's Hall.[28] The St Margaret's Street Quaker Meeting House then survived through the century but only just: by 1800 it had just one member, the building became disused soon after and remaining Quakers transferred to the Melksham meeting house.

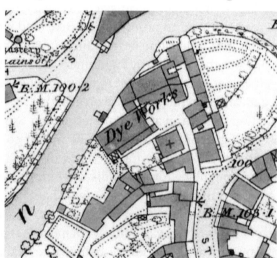

There is one other 18th century chapel to record, this one very much outside the mainstream of nonconformity: the Bearfield Chapel on what is now Huntingdon Street. It was opened in 1787 on the site of an old cloth warehouse. Nominally Independent, it held services according to the forms of the Church of England.[29] It survived in this form only a few years before closing, was then bought by one Posthumus Bush of Bradford who soon thereafter sold

1885 Ordnance Survey Map, the former Quaker meeting house marked with an added blue cross. The building between it and the river is now St Margaret's Hall

it on to the Revd Thomas Watkins of Bath. Watkins reopened the chapel, presumably with a similar form of worship, built a gallery and attracted a 'good and respectable congregation'. He died in 1802 and the complex continuing life of this chapel is described below.

Religion of the Majority – the 19th Century

A Century of Growth

An ecclesiastical census was carried out in 1851, prompted by a fear that overall church attendance was falling. In 1679 (see above) there were stated to be 159 dissenters in the town against 3105 conformists. On the census Sunday in 1851,[30] 1,800 people attended the morning or evening service, or both, at the two Church of England churches in the town; 2,740 attended one or both services at a nonconformist chapel. There were further local religious censuses in 1881 and the equivalent figures then for Bradford were: Church of England 1,566, nonconformist 2,566 (Baptist 1,011, Independent 655, Wesleyan Methodist 691, Primitive Methodist 209).[31]

No equivalent figures are available for the 18th century but almost all of this growth in nonconformist numbers would have come in the 19th. This left them in a clear majority by 1851, a position which was sustained through the rest of the century. In no part of England were nonconformists less than a third of total worshippers in 1851 but the average across the country was just under half whereas in Bradford it was 60% in 1851 and 62% in 1881.

What is the explanation for this remarkable growth, and for the notable strength of nonconformity here? Clearly much of the increase was down to the evangelical preaching of the Methodists and others and the remoteness and frequent indolence of the Anglican clergy, particularly in the earlier period. A further piece of evidence comes from comparing Bradford in 1851 with Marlborough, a town of similar size (population then 3,391 vs 3,836 for Bradford) but not a cloth town. The Marlborough Church of England clergy had reported little nonconformist activity in the town in response to the 1783 Visitation questions, in contrast to the vehement reply of the vicar of Holy Trinity.[32] On the 1851 census Sunday 2,000 people attended one or both services at the two parish churches in the town, against 1,028 attending nonconformist services. In other words, only 34% of worshippers in Marlborough were nonconformist.

It is hard to escape the conclusion that the key difference between these two towns, and the explanation for the large number of nonconformists in Bradford, was the support of the clothiers. In more traditional communities the power lay with the squire, and the squire was closely aligned with the parson: between them they could use their influence to ensure most parishioners remained loyal to the established church. But in the wool towns in the west of the county – and Bradford was not alone in this – the clothiers represented 'new money' and were nowhere near as closely tied to the previous hierarchy. They wielded equal if not more influence over their many workers and found the new and more dynamic religion of the nonconformists much to their taste.

Part of the strength of the nonconformists came from the realisation that to improve their position they needed to have links with other churches of the same persuasion. So the Quakers, despite their determinedly non-hierarchical structure, nevertheless set up a hierarchy of regular meetings covering increasingly large areas, to share information and advice. The Baptists also introduced area structures and as early as 1689 Baptists here sent deputies to the Baptist Assembly in London.[33] The Independents, mostly later Congregationalists, were nominally the most independent of the lot, yet they also realised the value of wider grouping: it was the Wilts and East Somerset Congregational Union which accepted the Bearfield chapel from the Countess of Huntingdon's Connexion in 1880, as noted below. Finally the Methodists from early on used the system of circuit preachers to allow a relatively small number of ministers to serve a large number of churches, each preaching at a different church in turn while lay preachers served those churches where there was no ordained minister on any particular Sunday. The ministers often ended up riding long distances on horseback but the system gave strength and support at a time when it was critically needed.

Existing chapels also directly sponsored new foundations, usually with practical and spiritual support and sometimes with money as well. Thus there is a suggestion that the Old Baptist was formed originally under the influence of Southwick Baptist, a major centre for Baptists in Wiltshire.[34] Much later two Bradford chapels sponsored others elsewhere: the small Baptist at Turleigh started independently of other churches in 1849 but struggled and was taken over c1870 by the Zion Baptist in Bradford;[35] and in 1892 the Bradford Leigh Methodist, an iron chapel, was built as a mission station of the Coppice Hill Methodist.[36]

Building a new chapel was a major undertaking and in many places the cost was such that work had to be delayed, often for many years. Corners were cut to save money and volunteer labour was often used. The support of the clothiers and other relatively wealthy people put Bradford in a different position to that of many places, as exemplified by the Morgan's Hill chapel of 1741 where the land was donated alongside gifts of £100 each from three people. No doubt not all were so fortunate as this group and the more general approach was to take out a loan, either from a wealthy local individual or later from organisations specially set up by the various denominations for this purpose. The Providence Baptist, for example (see below), having first borrowed the £100 cost of their building from a local benefactor, replaced that in 1867 with a loan from the Baptist Building Fund in London.[37]

In contrast to the obsessive checking which accompanies mortgage applications in the 21st century, many congregations simply set off on building their chapel, hoping for the best. Once the chapel was up, there were then vigorous attempts to raise money through assorted fund-raising activities. One example is provided by the Morgan's Hill Congregational where, planning improvements in 1913, the church had raised only £166 but went ahead anyway and let contracts for £336.[38] Paying loans back could take many years: the grand Coppice Hill Methodist of 1818 was particularly expensive to build, costing £7,000, and nearly 50 years later, in 1864, there was reported to be still £1,000 outstanding on the loan.[39] A tea party was being held to contribute towards the repayment.

Chapels also had to meet their running costs, not only for the building but also for the minister's salary. In several instances gifts were made of property, the rental income from which could be used for this purpose; so the Grove was endowed with houses at 18 and 19 Newtown in the 1780s,[40] the Old Baptist had had seven houses given by 1901,[41] and in 1796 Methodists had bought an acre of land at Woolley to help fund the Minister.[42]

Another source of income was charging pew rents, a practice also common in the Church of England and still in place well into the 20th century but now replaced by service collections and structured giving schemes. Most chapels had a mixture of free and rented pews – the free ones often in the gallery or other less desirable positions – and the dividing and numbering of pews, still to be seen clearly at the Bearfield Church, was a way of identifying which pew each family was renting. Chapel account books give some idea of the income from this source. At Morgan's Hill, for example, in 1856 19 families were paying pew rents of between 5/- and £2 per quarter, producing a total income of about £11 per quarter.[43] The minister's salary at that period was £35 a quarter so the church needed to earn substantial amounts more from other sources.

New Chapels

At the start of the 19th century Bradford had six nonconformist chapels. The Quaker Meeting House in the town centre was moribund and the Grove Meeting House was in decline under the long pastorship of Edward Williams (1777 to 1810).[44] But both the Morgan's Hill Independent and the St Margaret's Street Baptist seem to have been in good health. At the north end of town the Bearfield chapel was about to start on the next stage of its erratic journey to maturity and the Pippett Street Methodist was thriving.

Plenty more changes were to come this century, with more splitting of groups to record, but there were also four new chapels: a large new Methodist in the town centre, the Zion Baptist next to the Grove, a Primitive Methodist in Sladesbrook and a further Baptist chapel at the north end of Bearfield.

The first of the new chapels was the Coppice Hill Methodist, opened in 1818.[45] The Pippett Street Methodist was certainly not falling to bits – it is still in reasonably sound condition 200 years later – but its replacement was much larger, a reflection of how Methodism was prospering in the town.[46] By this date the Primitive Methodists had formed as a breakaway group, discussed further below in the context of their chapel at Sladesbrook, and the mainstream Methodist chapels like this one became known as Wesleyan Methodist. One source[47] says that the Methodists moved earlier

WHEREAS, it hath been duly certified to the Right Reverend Father in God, *John* by Divine Permission Lord Bishop of Salisbury, that *a certain Building situated in Upper Stoke*

in the Parish of *Bradford* in the County of *Wilts* and in his Lordship's Diocese *is intended forthwith to be used as a place of Religious Worship by an Assembly or Congregation of Protestants*

I do therefore hereby certify, that the same hath been registered and recorded in the Court of the said Lord Bishop, pursuant to the Directions of an Act of Parliament, passed in the fifty second year of the Reign of his late Majesty, King George the third, as Witness my Hand, this *Twenty Third* day of *February* in the year of our Lord, one thousand eight hundred and twenty *five*

Coppice Hill Methodist, registered for worship in 1825, some years after its first opening (WSA 1103/42)

than this, in 1790, to a chapel on Coppice Hill which was later replaced by that of 1818, but there seems to be no evidence to support this claim.[48] The Coppice Hill chapel was not quite the town's largest – both Morgan's Hill and the Old Baptist had greater capacity at the time of the 1851 ecclesiastical census – but its position on the hillside was a dominating one and it thrived throughout the rest of the century.

The next new chapel was the Zion Baptist, on the hillside directly alongside the Grove Meeting House where now there is a small car park. This came as the result of a further falling out. A group of people from the Morgan's Hill Independent, led by one William Coombs who had been invited to become pastor there but argued with the trustees, left that chapel in 1815. They then took a lease on the Grove chapel which by that date had ceased to function, the congregation having declined to zero.[49] It seems that many of those who left Morgan's Hill with Coombs returned there before long but nevertheless the remaining congregation was strong enough to build the Zion chapel, to which they moved in 1823.

The reason for building an additional chapel there is not clear. The Zion was larger than the Grove, with seats for 450, but surely such extra space was not needed at that early date: even at the time of the 1881 ecclesiastical census it was less than half full at both services.[50] But it could be that a smart new church was seen to symbolise the new religious life taking place there. The Grove was thereafter used for some years for a weekly meeting led by a minister from the Conigre Baptist in Trowbridge, another Unitarian church, but these meetings became increasingly infrequent until the Revd. Jones of Holy Trinity, writing in mid-century, was able to describe the chapel as 'fast hastening to decay', its covering of ivy giving it a 'singularly picturesque' appearance.[51]

Left: Zion Baptist, opposite the end of Middle Rank, in its later years
(Bradford on Avon Museum)

Below: Zion Baptist, formerly the Grove, the interior now much simplified

The members of the Zion chapel were joined in 1842 by a group who had seceded from the Old Baptist after another falling out, this time over the arrival of a 'Hyper-Calvinist' minister,[52] and the Zion chapel itself became Baptist almost immediately.[53] In 1873 it took over the Grove to use as a Sunday school and this opened after conversion in 1876.[54] In 1892 a further schoolroom and 'chapel keeper's house' were obtained by conversion of the adjacent house on Middle Rank, which retained a connecting door to the chapel until recent times.[55]

The Primitive Methodists had formed in 1810, driven by a belief that the main body of Methodists were moving away from the revivalist, 'primitive' style of John Wesley. They grew in strength rapidly and indeed much of the great growth in Methodism during the century was down to them rather than the Wesleyans.

Viewed as more working class than the Wesleyans, the Primitives may have had a presence in Bradford from when houses in Newtown and Bearfield were registered for worship in 1822 and 'a building in the occupation of William Brown' was registered in 1825.[56] The group was said to have formed under the influence of Primitive Methodists from Melksham and in 1845 opened the Sladesbrook Primitive Methodist chapel at the south end of Sladesbrook.[57] In 1851 at the time of the religious census it was attracting congregations of over 100 to its services but it was not to have a long life: it was still active in 1885 but was put up for auction in 1886 and by 1888 had been taken over as a hall for the Good Templars, a temperance organisation.[58]

Sladesbrook Primitive Methodist

The last of the new chapels was a third Baptist, the Providence Baptist Chapel in Bearfield Buildings just south of Ashley Road, opened in 1858.[59] This was made by

Providence Baptist Chapel before conversion back to housing
(Wiltshire Buildings Record)

converting two cottages, probably originally of the 18th century, in this long terrace. At this date Bearfield was both small in population and separated by Priory Park and the hillside from the town centre; not only that but there was already the Bearfield chapel nearby and the Zion chapel, also Baptist, was not much further away. This does make one wonder how it was thought a new chapel here, the third Baptist chapel in the town, would be justified. It did indeed have small congregations but nevertheless survived well into the 20th century.

The Providence chapel, like the Old Baptist in the town centre, was a 'Particular' as opposed to 'General' Baptist. The Zion chapel may have started as General but it too was Particular by the end of the 19th century if not before.[60] Particular Baptists believed in the Calvinist teaching that God had predestined only certain people for salvation and everyone else was doomed however good a life they led, whereas General Baptists believed everyone had the opportunity to secure personal salvation. To modern eyes the Calvinist doctrine might seem distinctly demotivating and in these ecumenical days such distinctions seem less important, but in previous centuries they were taken very seriously indeed and were the cause of frequent splits in congregations.

Such seriousness underlines the importance of religion in people's lives in the 19th century. The 1851 ecclesiastical census illustrates this by revealing what to our generation may seem staggeringly large numbers attending religious services. At the most well-attended service on census day, usually that held in the evening, the Old Baptist had 400 in the congregation, Morgan's Hill Independent 350 and Coppice Hill Wesleyan 360. Of the smaller chapels the Zion Baptist had 250 and even the Sladesbrook Primitive Methodist had 120. In total these numbers exceeded those of the Church of England churches, but these too had large numbers, Holy Trinity with 600 and Christ Church with 400.

These totals do not include children, of whom large numbers also attended if only for part of the service. Most chapels had separate rooms for Sunday schools, described in Chapter 3, and the combination of adults and children crowded into these not-huge interior spaces must have created an atmosphere in two senses of the word, and certainly added to the intensity of the religious experience.

Not the subject of this book, but the nonconformists were also active in weekday schooling. A system of 'British Schools' was introduced from 1808, intended to be non-denominational and to avoid what the nonconformists saw as the Church of England indoctrination taking place in most schools at that time: in 1817 the former Quaker meeting house in St Margaret's was adapted for this purpose. In the face of the perceived threat from nonconformity a society was formed in 1811 to promote more schools with Church of England teaching. These were the so-called 'National Schools,' one of which was erected in 1836 at the extreme west end of Church Street.[61]

Bearfield and the Countess of Huntingdon's Connexion

Most chapels were owned and managed by a group of trustees but the Bearfield Chapel had been in the ownership of one individual and remained so in the first two decades of the 19th century, the ownership passing between different ministers.[62] But at some date shortly before 1820 one of the joint owners, Henry Stroud, made over the chapel to 'Lady Huntingdon's Connexion.'

Selena, Countess of Huntingdon, was a rich widow after her husband died in 1746. An early supporter of Methodism, she used her money to fund Methodist ministers and often to build them chapels, choosing particularly those preachers who she believed would appeal to a middle to upper class audience.[63] She was also a believer in Calvinistic predestination, which put her in conflict with the Wesley brothers who were emphatically not, and led eventually to the formation of Lady Huntingdon's Connexion, a network of basically Methodist chapels with congregations tending towards the better off.

By the time the Bearfield chapel was made over to them, however, the Connexion had more or less lost its belief in predestination and the worship at Connexion chapels was generally Congregational. Nor was the congregation of the Bradford chapel affluent; indeed one minister left for America in 1844 because the small congregation could not afford to pay him a living wage.[64] A new minister took over in 1847 and brought some life but the congregation remained small and in 1879 the chapel was offered to the Wilts and East Somerset Congregational Union, which accepted it.[65] Thereafter it functioned as an independent Congregational church. Known originally as the Bethel chapel, it became known as the Countess of Huntingdon's chapel in the 1820s, a name which stuck well past the date at which it became Congregational; indeed it was still often called that as late as the 1930s.[66]

The Established Chapels

The Quaker meeting had ceased to exist by the start of the new century; their meeting house at Cumberwell was sold in 1813[67] and that by St Margaret's was soon to have other uses, including as a British School. There seem to have been occasional Quaker meetings in their meeting house but these did not lead to the re-establishment of a permanent Quaker congregation.[68] The Grove, superseded by the new Zion chapel, regained some life towards the century's end as a Sunday school.

Elsewhere the Morgan's Hill Independent suffered a crisis after the minister and a group of members left it in 1815. Resolving this was painful but the result was that the excessive power of the trustees was broken and this set the chapel on a century of prosperity. The building was extended again in 1835 to accommodate a growing congregation and a schoolroom was added. Before the 1836 Marriage Act all marriages had had to take place in the Church of England but that Act made it possible for nonconformist chapels, amongst others, to be licensed to conduct

SOCIETY OF FRIENDS.

The Inhabitants of

BRADFORD-ON-AVON

are cordially invited to attend

A MEETING

FOR DIVINE WORSHIP

To be held in the

FRIENDS MEETING HOUSE,

(Technical School Laboratory)

NEAR ST. MARGARET STREET, ON

TUESDAY, SEP. 25th, 1894,

at Eight p.m.

Several Ministers and other Friends intend to
be present at the Meeting.

NO COLLECTION.

C. RAWLING, PRINTER, BRADFORD-ON-AVON.

Occasional Quaker meetings in the late 19th century seem not to have led to anything greater (WSA 1273/10)

weddings. Morgan's Hill was so licensed in 1837[69] and the Old Baptist a year later.[70]

By the late 1850s Morgan's Hill was known as a Congregational chapel, in the way that almost all Independent chapels changed titles, but the exact date of changing is not known and there was probably little alteration in the way services were conducted.[71]

The Old Baptist had the largest congregation of any nonconformist church in the town in mid-century[72] and was prosperous enough to undertake a major restoration in 1887.[73] There are some signs, however, that attendance at the church was in decline by the end of the century.[74]

Lastly, two other groups should be mentioned, the first being the Salvation Army, founded in London in 1865. There seems not to have been a group in Bradford but the Trowbridge contingent, formed in 1880,[75] were soon sending their members to Bradford, marching and singing through the town. They were not well received, being repeatedly attacked by local youths, but seem to have persisted in this action until at least 1890.[76] They had a mission room in The Square, towards the east end of St Margaret's Hill where now there are two blocks of garages, but this was sold in 1915, by which date it seems likely that they had not been active in Bradford for some years.[77]

The second group is the Catholic Apostolic church, which is said to have had a congregation of members in Bradford in 1836.[78] This church was formed in London at the start of the 1830s and was made up of people whose evangelical preaching took them out of the Church of England, though in contrast to other nonconformists they retained most of the trappings of the established church. It seems unlikely that the Catholic Apostolic church in Bradford ever had its own premises but they had a church in Bath, in place by 1851 when it recorded 110 people at its main service on the day of the ecclesiastical census.[79] Evangelists from this church came to Bradford and other Wiltshire towns in the 1870s, giving weekly lectures here in the town hall,[80] and returned to Trowbridge, and perhaps Bradford as well, in 1897.[81]

Contraction – the 20th Century and Beyond

The decline in church attendance, affecting the Church of England and nonconformist churches alike, started around the turn of the century but was accelerated by the First World War. The causes have been much debated but we do now live in an age when church attendance is the exception rather than the norm. As a result, in Bradford only four of the six chapels operating at the start of the 20th century remain open. These are the Old Baptist, Morgan's Hill Congregational (now the United Church), Zion (now back using the former Grove meeting house) and the Countess of Huntingdon's (now the Bearfield Church). Despite the negative background, all four appear to be in good shape.

The Quakers re-established

The Quakers, more recently, have increased that number to five. They had ceased to function in the town by the beginning of the 19th century but made an attempt to re-establish themselves in 1894, holding a meeting in their old meeting house, attended by 60 and said to be the first in the town for 50 years.[82] These efforts seem not to have met with any continuing success, however, and Bradford Quakers in the 20th century relied on meetings in Trowbridge until in the 1960s they decided a move back to Bradford could be sustained if they could find suitable premises.[83] The choice fell on a house in Whitehead's Lane, previously associated with Spencer's Brewery; they eventually bought this, following many delays, in 1970. After a considerable amount of renovation they brought it into use as a meeting house, the meeting room on the ground floor. Whitehead's Lane, appropriately enough, is named after Manasseh Whitehead, a Quaker banker who lived there in the late 17th century.[84] The Quakers have operated from these premises ever since.

The new Quaker meeting house on Whitehead's Lane

Three Chapels Closed

The Sladesbrook Primitive Methodist had closed just before the end of the previous century. The three chapels which closed in the 20th century all lasted until after the Second World War, first to go being the Zion Baptist. The fabric of this chapel had been deteriorating and in 1939 the congregation moved back into the Grove building of 1698, transferring the Zion name to the old chapel. The original chapel was requisitioned for the Red Cross during the War, which did little for its condition, and it was used for some years afterwards for storage before being sold in 1953 and demolished a few years later, probably in the early 1960s. The site was subsequently converted into a small car park.

The Coppice Hill Wesleyan Methodist was the next to go. It was a grand and impressive building but with equally grand maintenance costs. The declining congregation found these too much to afford and in the late 1950s, perhaps 1959, moved into the schoolroom, a separate building in the chapel's forecourt described in Chapter 3.[86] They stayed here until 1976 but in that year abandoned the whole site and combined with the Morgan's Hill Congregational, which itself had been redesignated as a United Reformed Church following the 1972 national union of Congregationalists and Presbyterians.[87] The two congregations shared services but remained otherwise distinct for a period but then combined into what was thereafter known as the United Church. The subsequent history of the Coppice Hill building is described in the next chapter.

Last to go, perhaps surprisingly, was the tiny Providence Baptist at Bearfield. This remained buoyant for much of the first half of the century, celebrating a new schoolroom twice the size of the old one in 1933,[88] but post-war decline led eventually to its closure in the early 1980s. It was auctioned in 1989[89] and then converted back into two houses. The pulpit and one of the pews are on display in the Bradford on Avon museum

Coppice Hill Methodist, derelict in 1967 (RCHME)

The Established Chapels

The Old Baptist went through a difficult period at the start of the century. The minister left in 1903 because the church could no longer afford to pay him, and it declined further until in the 1930s it had tiny congregations and the building was in dire need of renovation.[90] Many assumed it would close but the arrival of a couple from Chippenham, the Alsops, led to a steady recovery. The number of members increased, the Sunday school, which had closed in 1912, was reopened in 1947, and renovations were carried out.[91] This trend, once started, has continued to the present day.

The Morgan's Hill Congregational had renovations and improvements through the 20th century, for example re-seating in 1913 to replace the box pews, reconstruction of the organ in 1926 and a series of redecorations and other improvements.[92] The church joined the new United Reform Church in 1972 and combined with the Methodists in 1976 to become thereafter the United Church, as noted above. It has continued to prosper since.

The major event for the Zion Church during the 20th century was the move back to the former Grove meeting house at the time of the Second World War and the subsequent demolition of the Zion chapel. Since then the church appears to have continued with a small but sustained congregation.

The Bearfield Church continued active through the 20th century, with various alterations and improvements to the buildings which are noted in the following chapter. It did not join the Congregational Union in 1972, remaining completely independent, but its ministry continues.

3 The Buildings – Testaments in Stone

A note on Chapel Design

Our image of a nonconformist chapel might be of a gable-ended building, the door central, windows symmetrically placed and perhaps a plaque with the date and chapel name top central. Such an image would not be wrong – many if not most do look like this – but there are plentiful variations to be found as the descriptions below should illustrate.

The Old Baptist, interior view from gallery

The Old Baptist, interior looking towards the entrance

Chapel interiors, however, followed a remarkably uniform set of rules from the beginning, defined by the underlying purpose of their design. This was to create a 'preaching box.' Ancient parish churches were designed for Catholic worship, the mysteries of the chancel and the rituals of the priest at the altar separated from the congregation in the nave, often physically so by a rood screen. Nonconformists wanted none of this ritual: for them, listening to the word of the preacher was the central purpose of their attendance at worship.

So when we look at a chapel interior like that of the Old Baptist in Bradford the first thing to strike us may be the pulpit, centrally placed and raised up so that the preacher can command both the floor of the church and the gallery. Galleries, here supported on cast iron columns, bring the congregation closer to the preacher and there is no altar, just a communion table in front of the pulpit. The pulpit has two stairways up to it, quite unnecessarily since it will only accommodate one person at a time but symbolising a second major characteristic of nonconformist chapels and that is their commitment to symmetry. Look at this interior and it is hard to spot anything which is not either centrally placed or in symmetrical pairs: the pews, the rear windows now blocked off because an extension was built beyond, the doors, even the twin sets of stairs giving access to the gallery.

Monks chapel, Corsham, interior

Other points are worth noting. Originally all the replaced pews would have been box pews, as this illustration of the 1690 interior of the Monks chapel at Corsham, a rare early survivor, shows. But almost all chapels, and indeed Church of England churches, had these replaced by open pews in the 19th century. Here the gallery retains box pews but those below were replaced in renovations in 1887. Also the present-day interior is immaculate and brightly painted but this was almost certainly not the case in earlier years when the woodwork was probably just stained and modern paints were not available to produce the bright white of the walls; they were instead often covered with painted biblical quotations in curving scrolls. It is worth noting also that nonconformist chapels are almost always devoid of stained glass since such decoration was considered to be close to idolatry. Only in the late 19th century, such as in Bradford in the Morgan's Hill Congregational, was some coloured glass intruded and even then the designs used were unobtrusive and usually patterned rather than figurative.

There is a lobby at the entrance end, a later addition though neatly done. Such additions were common: chapels were often built with the doors opening straight to the outside, but a few winters of howling draughts were usually enough to persuade them that separation by means of a lobby was required. Finally, the view looking towards the rear of the church shows the clock attached to the gallery front: this one is modern but they were a feature from early times, fixed in this position so that the preacher could tell how long he had been preaching for. Most of the congregation, whose minds should have been on higher things than the passing time, could not see it.

This is a Baptist church and so needed a place for adult baptisms. Initially these were carried out in the river at Barton Bridge and attended by large numbers of people[93] but late in the century a tank was created in front of the pulpit, covered during normal times, a change common for Baptist churches in this period and with obvious advantages.[94] This feature distinguished Baptist churches from those of other denominations but it was barely evident and generally it would be hard to tell a Baptist chapel interior from that of a Congregationalist or a Methodist. Only the Quakers, with no ministers and hence no need for a pulpit, had distinctively different interiors.

In the late 17th and 18th centuries the Church of England, Protestantism now firmly established, rethought the design of its own new churches to reflect the reduced emphasis on ritual and an increase in the importance given to preaching. Wren's city churches in London were an early example of this style, producing a single large space without a separate chancel, often with galleries on three sides in much the same style as was being adopted by the nonconformists. James Gibbs' St Martin's in the Fields of 1724 is perhaps the most famous example, much more heavily ornamented than any nonconformist chapel but with the same basic layout.

But the new Church of England style fell foul of the Oxford Movement in the 19th century, with its High Church practices. In a local example, Christ Church in Bradford was built in 1839-41 in Gothic Revival style but with a plain interior and no chancel, very much a 'preaching box'. But it succumbed to Sir George Gilbert Scott in 1878[95] and ended up with just the same chancel, rood screen and the like as its medieval predecessors. In more recent years many Church of England churches, Holy Trinity in Bradford one of them, have reversed the trend and brought the altar and communion rail forward to the crossing to take the service closer to the congregation.

So the layout of Anglican churches has often changed through the years but Nonconformist chapels have remained remarkably consistent. Many have now replaced pews by chairs to give more flexibility in layout, and of course they now have better heating and electric light, but the modern Nonconformist church has essentially the same layout as the Bradford Old Baptist of 1797 or indeed the Monk's Lane chapel at Corsham from the very start of chapel building in 1690.

Right: Christ Church as built, a 'preaching box' (Bradford on Avon museum)

Bradford on Avon Museum

Below: Christ Church now, as rebuilt in 1878

Finally, there is the question of who designed these chapels. We will look in vain for a named architect for most of them: the carpenter Robert Cadby may have been responsible for the design of the 1798 extension of the Morgan's Hill Congregational[96] and a Mr Evans designed the Coppice Hill Methodist, but we cannot be certain which Evans out of several possibilities with that name. Otherwise we know only the names of a few of the stonemasons and carpenters who worked on them. This should not be a surprise, however, for the overlap between craftsmen and architects was substantial until recent times. Poorer congregations in particular would have struggled to afford the services of an architect when an experienced mason or carpenter, with plenty of knowledge of other buildings elsewhere, could produce them a good design. By the late 19th century architects were much to the fore – T B Silcock for example at Bearfield in 1892 and Alfred Long, from West Bromwich but a member of a Bradford on Avon family of builders, after the century's end in 1913 at Morgan's Hill.[97]

Quaker Meeting Houses in Bradford

The location of the Cumberwell Quaker Meeting House, believed to have been built first in 1676 but soon rebuilt, is uncertain. The general location is identified by the Victoria County History and a map of 1773.[98] It is believed to have been still standing in 1859, by then in use as a school,[99] and the 1841 tithe map shows only one pair of buildings in a likely position, corresponding approximately to the rear of what are now 119 and 120 Bath Road, two of a terrace of three houses. There is no obvious evidence of such previous use in the two houses but No.119 is called 'Old Chapel House' and this location is suggested as that of the meeting house by at least one source.[100] It appears to be the most likely place.

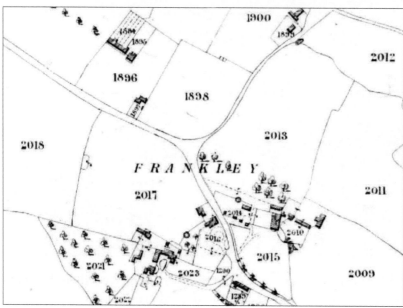

1841 tithe map showing at No.1897 the most likely location of the first Quaker meeting house. Potticks House is at the front of No.1895

The Quakers were not here long for in 1718, no doubt encouraged by the more tolerant national regime now in place, they built a new meeting house in a much less inconspicuous location in the town centre. The Cumberwell meeting house seems to have continued in some use – the 1773 map marks it as such – and the associated burial ground did not receive its last burial until 1803.[101] The meeting house itself was sold in 1813.[102]

Coming into the car park by St Margaret's Hall now, it is hard to realise how different this place is from what it was within living memory. Then there was just a small courtyard, completely surrounded by industrial buildings including ranges backing onto both the river and Westbury Gardens. St Margaret's Hall, originally a dye house, was just one of these buildings and the former St Margaret's Street Quaker Meeting House was another. It was located more or less where there are now two rows of car parking spaces south of the hall. The meeting house itself was at the east end, close to Westbury House, and the burial ground stretched out behind it to the west. It was said to have seated 170, so was of modest size.[103] Surprisingly, for a building in the town centre which was not demolished until recent times, there seems to be almost no record of its appearance. An aerial photograph, of poor quality, indicates only tall side windows and a hipped roof perhaps of 'double pile' form.

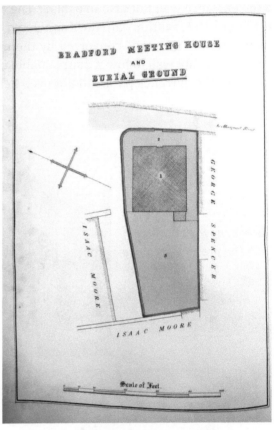

After the meeting closed at the end of the 18th century the last burial was in 1803.[104] The meeting house was for long disused but by 1825 was taken over as a British (nonconformist) school.[105] This eventually closed in the 1880s by which time the building was in a poor state.[106] It was thereafter sold in 1902, used for storage and finally demolished in the 1960s to make way for the car park.[107]

St Margaret's Quaker meeting house; the burial ground was west of the building (WSA1699/104)

From the beginning of the 19th century there was virtually no Quaker presence in the town until the new meeting house on Whitehead's Lane opened in 1971. This is a building of the 1870s which had been associated with the former Spencer's brewery. The three-bay house, gabled at one end, faces the lane with round-arched windows on two floors, but the ground floor meeting room, converted when the building was bought, is accessed from the rear.

The Grove and Zion Chapels

The **Grove Baptist** chapel of 1698 was so-called because there was previously a grove of alders on the slopes here.[108] Now called the Zion Baptist, it faces Conigre Hill, the door central below a large mullioned and transomed window, the whole beneath a hipped tile roof which is in fact a double pile, two ridges running east to west in parallel. But pause a moment and you will notice something incongruous, for the wall here is of rough stone, commonly used at this time for the side and rear walls of a building, whereas the long south-facing wall is of smooth ashlar. So why is the entrance wall not also in ashlar? The answer is that this was not an entrance at all until 1876; at this date the dilapidated chapel, transferred to the Zion chapel's ownership in 1874, was converted by them into a schoolroom.[109] Before that date this was a blank wall below a double-gabled, not hipped, roof[110] and the land to the east, now the entrance path, did not even belong to the church.[111]

*Grove, now Zion, chapel,
the present entrance*

*Grove, now Zion, chapel,
the original entrance
front*

So we should look instead at the original entrance front, which is much more interesting. This is of six bays with doors either end, the windows mullioned and transomed apart from a round-arched central pair at first floor level. The composition is harmonious and also remarkably bold, looking out from its conspicuous position above the town at a date when nonconformity was barely tolerated: another illustration of how strong the protection of the clothiers must have been.

The chapel was of the 'long wall' type, orientated not in the conventional way as it is now with the pulpit on the narrow end but rather with it at the centre of one of the long walls, probably the front one since the chapel was built also with galleries running round three sides.[112] The central valley of the roof was held up by wooden columns – removed when the original stone slate roof was replaced by lighter tiles in 1876[113] - and the whole interior must have provided an intimate, perhaps almost claustrophobic, space when full of worshippers.

The fate of almost all 'long wall' chapels was to be converted to a conventional layout, for the preacher would have had difficulty in commanding the congregation spread so widely in front of him and buildings of this type needed much more of the expensive street-frontage land than the alternative. The Grove had to wait until 1876 for the physical changes to be made, although by that time it was in any case not a functioning chapel. Its role as a schoolroom was evidently successful because in 1892 the adjacent house on Middle Rank was purchased and converted into a further schoolroom as well as accommodation for the chapel-keeper.[114]

The chapel is now stripped out and simply furnished, only the Gothic organ from the demolished Zion chapel standing out. The doors to the front are not used; a door through to the adjacent house is also blocked off as is one to the rear into what used to be a passage but was filled in when the land behind began to give way. The chief interest remains the building's structure, harmonious in both its proportions and its detail and a remarkable testament to the early commitment of nonconformists in Bradford.

It is a shame that there is no better image available of the Zion Baptist

Zion chapel (Bradford on Avon Museum)

of 1823, for it seems to have been a handsome building: as with the St Margaret's Quaker meeting house, it is surprising that a building demolished only in quite recent times is so little recorded. The design was typical of its time, the front of three bays with a rusticated ground floor and ashlar stone above. The windows, one each side of the door and three above, were round-arched with intersecting glazing bars; the central bay was drawn forward slightly and topped with a pediment within which was an inscription giving the chapel's name and the date; a flat cornice stretched across the other bays.

To the rear of the modern car park is a substantial retaining wall, showing how far the hillside had to be cut away to accommodate the chapel. It was clearly of some length, though it seems there were also schoolrooms to the rear.[115] Now there is no trace left except for the iron railings at the front overlooking the town.

The Old Baptist

The Old Baptist is a hidden chapel, its presence obvious enough from the inscription over the archway leading to it but the building itself scarcely visible; indeed the best view of it is to be had not from here at all but from high up on the hillside to the north. Its predecessor was accessed off Morgan's (now St Margaret's) Hill, probably from immediately north of 1 St Margaret's Hill, which is believed to be 17th century[116] and so likely pre-dates the chapel. However, when they came to rebuild in 1797 they bought the house in front, a good symmetrical 18th century town house of ashlar stone, and drove a passageway through where previously there had been the right hand pair of ground floor windows. Most of the house was thereafter used for schoolrooms.

Street entranceway to the Old Baptist in the early 20th century
(Bradford on Avon Museum)

The same in 2024

The exterior of the chapel is almost as harmonious as the interior, described above. The front is in ashlar but the sides and rear in rubblestone; the roof is hipped and the roof angle steep so that it is almost pyramidal. The windows, in two tiers

Above: Old Baptist, side view with vestry to rear

*Right: Old Baptist, blocked-in
former door in front wall*

above and below the galleries, have two-centred segmental arches with Y tracery and to the rear a large lean-to vestry mostly covers what had been a pair of similar but taller windows in the rear wall of the church. The front wall has blocked-in doors to either side, probably original but uncomfortably positioned in relation to the windows here. These simple efforts were later replaced by a larger central door with Tuscan columns and a pediment.

The remaining space behind the chapel and to the north was formerly a burial ground. There have been numerous alterations and refurbishments over the more than two centuries of continuous use for this building, including not only the removal of the box pews but also, for example, a new heating system in 1914 and removal of two rows of pews to allow the vestibule to be expanded in 1989.[117] It remains, however, a building of remarkable integrity, giving a strong sense of how nonconformist worship was conducted in times past.

Morgan's Hill Congregational, now the United Church

The Morgan's Hill church is now more visible than its near neighbour the Old Baptist but this was not the case until the 1960s. Until then there was continuous building from the end of the schoolroom on St Margaret's Hill to the corner and along St Margaret's Street to where the path leads up to the church.[118] The mark of the roofline of what was the chapel keeper's house[119] is still visible on the schoolroom and further houses on the far side blocked the view of the rear of the chapel. All were demolished, but the entrance gate pillars with their ornate metal overthrow lamp bracket still give a sense of separation from the street.

Entrance to Morgan's Hill chapel c1960, showing how enclosed it formerly was
(Bradford on Avon museum)

Morgan's Hill chapel, side view showing the quoin stones of the 1798 extension

The chapel, now exposed in this way, shows plenty of its history in the outside fabric, the main fronts of which are in ashlar, the remainder in coursed rubblestone. As built its proportions must have been not far from those of the Grove chapel: it had the same width as now but was much less deep, making it almost a chapel of the 'long wall' type.[120] The first extension was in 1798[121] when the chapel was extended back by 12 feet, making it almost square, and the quoin stones of that first rebuilding are still visible on the side walls.[122] Then in 1835 there was a further extension back for yet more space, the seating capacity increased to 650. At the same time the roof was raised by 4ft, still hipped but with tiles replaced by slates. It is not clear why the extra height was thought necessary since the headroom above the gallery seating must have been already generous, but perhaps it was done just to improve further the grandeur of the building.

These changes left the chapel front with much of its present rather uncomfortable appearance. Previous doors were blocked in, as was a central window on the first floor which has, strangely, a wooden lintel. A new central doorcase was inserted, with pilasters and a small pediment above, and there were two flat-headed windows either side on each of the two floors. Above is perhaps the strangest feature, a string course above the upper windows raised into the impression of a pediment at the centre, contained within which is an oval plaque giving the chapel's dates of building and extension. An external lobby was added, perhaps also in 1835, but this was removed and replaced by an internal one in 1892.

Two other buildings complete the picture. Immediately to the left of the chapel is an attached two-storey construction in ashlar with a lean-to roof, the front at a level with the chapel's string course: this was probably built as the minister's house originally and could well be a product also of the 1835 alterations. The much larger schoolroom building, the front also in ashlar, projects at right angles beyond that. This was altered or enlarged in 1850. The doorcases of all three doors here are identical, perhaps all added in the 1835 works.

Morgan's Hill chapel, the substantial schoolroom prominent to the left hand side. Note mark of roofline of previous building still visible at the left hand end of the schoolroom.

Morgan's Hill chapel, interior, the modest stained glass added at a late date.

The chapel interior is grand, with galleries on three sides on wooden columns and a curved ceiling making full use of the extra 4ft of height. Pews remain in the gallery, with its panelled fronts, but those below have been replaced by chairs. The windows are flat-headed bar the two behind the pulpit which are segmentally arched, and these and a few others contain some stained glass imagery, probably dating from renovations carried out in 1913 and further evidence for how long it was before nonconformists would accept this form of decoration. There is more stained glass in the end windows of the main schoolroom, now the church hall.

Early dissenters were much opposed to music in church services but that position softened over time and by the 19th century many chapels had harmoniums and the better off had begun to afford organs. This caused a problem, since organs were bulky instruments and there was often nowhere to put one without destroying the symmetry which was considered so important. Many compromised and put the organ as unobtrusively as possible in a corner, but Morgan's Hill, which may have obtained its organ c1850,[123] followed the pattern of many other larger chapels and placed

Morgan's Hill chapel, interior looking to the rear and showing the organ

it centrally in the rear gallery, thereby making an imposing addition to the interior without destroying the symmetry. It is possible that the central first floor window was blocked in when the organ was acquired, since the instrument would anyway have obstructed all light from it.

The near neighbours – Old Baptist and Morgan's Hill Congregational – invite comparison. The Old Baptist has been altered less over the years and its interior presents a more intimate appearance. Morgan's Hill, though, is certainly the town's grandest chapel now that the Coppice Hill Methodist is no more, and its much-altered exterior tells the story of its many changes in an engaging way.

View over the town showing the Old Baptist and Morgan's Hill chapels, distinguished by their hipped roofs. The Old Baptist is the nearer and smaller of the two

The Bearfield Church

The old stone terraces of Huntingdon Street give us a charming glimpse of bygone Bradford and the Bearfield chapel fits admirably into these surroundings. The chapel is simple vernacular architecture of the late 18th century, three bays of coursed rubblestone facing the street under a hipped roof of graduated stone slates, with three flat-headed windows and the legend 'Bearfield Church' above the central one. This is the side of the building: the front faces a side path and here there are two similar windows and a third, round-arched, high up above the door. A later porch projects forwards and to the front of this is attached a Classical doorway, complete with pilasters and pediment, which is out of sympathy with the rest of the building.

Bearfield Church, showing the entrance front, schoolroom to the rear. See also image on front cover.

This is but a small blot on an otherwise harmonious whole, however, and the inside is equally simple and straightforward. The room is tall and well lit, even though two walls are almost windowless. There is a lobby made of pine, the walls are panelled to waist height and the pews are numbered, the central set asymmetrically divided to allow the different families' pews to be differentiated and also presumably to give greater stability to what are very long benches. The pulpit is of modest size, its curving front in wrought iron patterns with an Art Nouveau feel.

Bearfield Church interior looking towards the entrance

The lobby, pews, panelling and the like were all the work of the Bath architect T B Silcock in 1892, intended to update and renew the chapel interior.[124] More puzzling is what was there before, for the chapel was built with a gallery, in which an organ was installed in 1850,[125] and this gallery was removed as part of the 1892 works. Such a gallery would inevitably have cut across the windows had these been in their present position but there seems to be no evidence that the windows were altered in 1892. Perhaps the gallery always obstructed them.

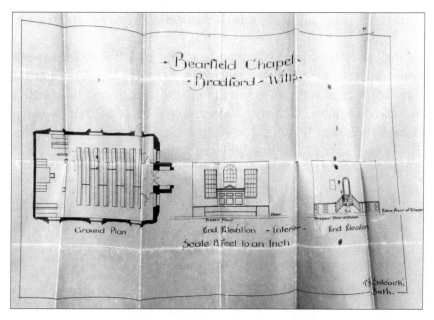

Bearfield Church, Silcock's plans for the 1892 alterations showing the simple interior (WSA1418/9)

Attached to the left hand side of the chapel, observed from the road, is a single storey bow-fronted lean-to building in ashlar. This is the minister's house, built originally as two storeys plus a basement by the Rev. Thomas Watkins from Bath, who had bought the chapel c1800.[126] At around the same time as the 1892 renovations the minister's house ceased to be used as such and instead was turned into schoolrooms. In 1925 the building was in such a poor state that it was reduced to its present height.[127] At the same date the main schoolroom, projecting at right angles to the rear of the chapel, was enlarged and rebuilt to create the three-bay extension which remains, in stone block under a tiled roof.[128] The space thus created is now a single large and well-lit room.

There used to be three large stone eagles in the chapel, two with holes drilled to take the supports for a communion rail and the third supporting the reading desk.[129] These symbolic figures were much used in Countess of Huntingdon chapels – the chapel in Bath, now the Museum of Bath Architecture, still retains one – and those in Bradford were installed soon after the chapel was made over to the Countess of Huntingdon's Connexion.[130] The Bradford eagles seem now to have disappeared.[131]

Wesleyan Methodists at Pippett Street and Coppice Hill

If the Old Baptist is a hidden church what about the Pippett Street Methodist, whose existence it would be unlikely anyone would guess at without the benefit of prior knowledge? Entirely hidden behind the Market Street frontage, now the Stumble Inn, the presence of the chapel is betrayed in aerial photographs only by the row of three parallel hipped pantiled roofs covering a substantial rectangular space.

Richard Pearce re-fronted the Maidenhead Inn in 1755, to give it much of its present appearance,[132] although the attic storey seems to be a later addition. It is of good ashlar in four bays and two storeys plus attic, the ground floor with a door to the left then three round-arched and pilastered openings: the first two are windows and the last is over a door leading to a side passage. Above a moulded string course are four flat-arched sashed windows and the attic has three dormers in a mansard roof.

29 Market Street when in use as Rawling's printing works, the post office next door (Bradford on Avon museum)

The same building now; the original entrance to the Methodist chapel was through the right hand archway

It seems that the chapel, built on the site of a former malthouse, was originally accessed via the side passage, with a doorway into the building immediately behind the Inn.[133] Though unconventional in position and external shape the chapel interior was

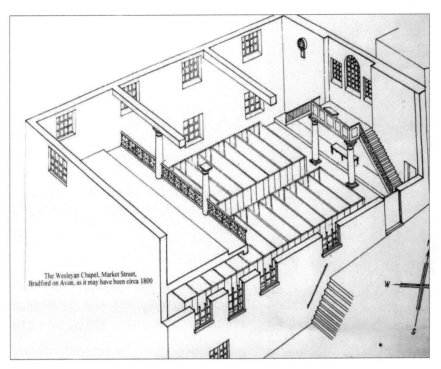

The Wesleyan Chapel, Market Street,
Bradford on Avon, as it may have been circa 1800

Pippett Street Methodist, conjectural plan of chapel interior
(Bradford on Avon Club)

consistent with the practice of the time: there was a rear gallery supported on substantial timber columns which also held up one of the two cross-beams supporting the valleys of the roof – there may well have been columns holding up the other cross-beam also – and the pulpit was raised with stairs up on either side. The walls were of rubblestone, the windows rectangular except for a substantial Venetian window behind the pulpit, and to the rear were both the minister's house and a small burial ground. Still retained in the clubrooms in front is the clock said to be that which Wesley preached in front of.

By 1802 the access is believed to have changed to one through the Inn,[134] an unlikely route for the Methodists to use and perhaps lending support to the claim by one source, noted in Chapter 2, that they moved out of this chapel in 1790. In any event, the rising ground behind the Inn required a flight of stairs to be climbed to reach the chapel, which was afterwards used first by Rawling's printing works and later by the Town Club. It is now used as a billiards room, the windows blocked, most of the fittings removed but the gallery with its columns still in place. There is a suspended ceiling inserted over the rest of the space at gallery level. The wrought iron tracery on the gallery front also survives, but in a style which looks later and so suggests that the afterlife of this building was possibly more prosperous in its days as part of the Town Club than might have been supposed.

Left: Pippett Street Methodist, the gallery front before insertion of a ceiling at first floor level (RCHME)

Right: Pippett Street Methodist, rear ¾ view of this hidden building, showing the distinctive three-part roof and Venetian window at back

The Coppice Hill chapel is splendid. Even now, when it is just an empty shell, it stands out on the hillside like the ruin of some great Tuscan villa. The architect of this fine building is not certain: it is believed to have been a Mr Evans but this might be T L Evans of London or perhaps Daniel Evans of Oxford, who had built the Methodist chapel in that city the previous year.[135] Whichever it was, he produced a bold and handsome façade very different from the timid and hidden efforts which so often characterised nonconformist chapel building of a century before.

Coppice Hill Methodist, derelict in the late 1960s (Wiltshire Buildings Record)

Coppice Hill Methodist, the shell still prominent in the view from the town centre

The monumental front is of five bays, the central three stepped forward, with two tiers of large round-arched windows below a pedimented three-bay attic with giant scrolls either side. The doorway, equally assertive, has Tuscan columns with a frieze and pediment. The sides also have two tiers of similarly shaped windows and at the back an apse-shaped extension, taking up the equivalent of three bays width, provided space for organ and choir.

The interior, seating over 600,[136] was on an equally large scale: a deep gallery with tiered seating stretched round three sides, the end curved in a semicircle, and the pulpit with choir stalls behind it dominated the far end. The design was greatly admired, so much so that the Manvers Street Wesleyan in Trowbridge of 1836, now

Coppice Hill Methodist, the interior impressive even when photographed in dereliction in 1967 (RCHME)

demolished, was based closely on this chapel. The Coppice Hill chapel was designed for a large congregation and it was no surprise that, with much smaller numbers worshipping in the post-war period, it was seen as a burden and was abandoned. Perhaps if this change had happened even ten years later this grand building might have been saved in its entirety, but as it is we are fortunate that a deal was eventually done with a neighbour who bought the chapel, demolished everything but the external walls and built a swimming pool in the interior space.

Manvers Street Wesleyan, Trowbridge, said to have been modelled on that in Bradford (RCHME)

Two footnotes may be added to the description of this chapel. Firstly, its position half way up the hill might have meant that, to reach it, worshippers from the north of the town would have had to walk down to the town centre then back up Coppice Hill. But this tiring problem was averted by providing a direct path from off a side turning high up Masons Lane. The gate posts, gates and overthrow lamp holder are still there, 'To the Chapel' inscribed on one of the pillars, the wording on the other now indecipherable.

Coppice Hill Methodist shell in 2024, schoolhouse to the right
(Hamptons estate agents)

Secondly, the Sunday school should be noted, for it is a handsome building of the mid-19th century,[137] of six bays in ashlar, the windows round-arched and with a substantial double-pilastered porch. It was to here that the congregation moved after abandoning the chapel in the late 1950s. It is now a private house.

Late Arrivals

Sladesbrook Primitive Methodist and the Providence Baptist

The chapels in the town centre are all relatively large and clearly 'town chapels', but the Sladesbrook Primitive Methodist has much the look of a typical village chapel of the mid-19th century, though its windows are more generously sized than many. The three windows and door on the ashlar front façade are all round-arched, with tall ones either side of the door and a smaller one over it. Above these is a cornice with a pediment which has the date of construction – 1845 – inscribed at the very top and below that a larger stone plaque, no doubt originally proclaiming the name of the chapel in the usual fashion but now erased. The sides, in stone blockwork of lesser quality, each have a flat-headed window and the north side shows in the rubble stone construction towards the rear where another house, now demolished, was formerly attached to it.[138] The chapel, which had a short and not very successful life, appears never to have had a schoolroom built on or any other alterations made.

Sladesbrook Primitive Methodist, side view showing where another building was previously joined to the rear. (Front view in Chapter 2)

In after life it was used for a period by the 'Good Templars'[139] and later served as extra accommodation for Christchurch School before the new school was built.[140] It was then converted into a house. In doing so the converters faced the common problem that former chapels are usually tall spaces into which it is necessary to insert an intermediate floor to create a viable house. But the main windows were often equally tall so inserting a floor would cut across the windows. Many, as here, split the windows into two, a thick panel showing where the inserted floor is: this creates unattractive window framing. The alternative, used in many more recent conversions, is to maintain the original windows and cut short the new floor inside them. The Sladesbrook chapel also originally had a fanlight above the double doors[141] but this has been replaced by boarding, with detrimental effect.

Next to the Providence Baptist in Bearfield Buildings are terraced cottages in stone blockwork of probably 18th century date, and we must assume that the chapel looked much like these before its conversion in 1858. In the conversion the Baptists took out the middle floor to create a single tall space with a small gallery at the right hand end supported on a cross-beam and a pair of closely spaced columns. Three tall new round-arched windows were created to light the main space and at the right hand end a single round-arched door was placed beneath a smaller window. Above the fanlight 'Providence Baptist Chapel' was incised in the stonework and this wording remains.

Inside were nine pews on each side of an aisle – a modest capacity although there was additional space in the gallery – and a pulpit of Gothic design which is now to be found, with one of the pews, in the Bradford on Avon museum.[142] An entrance lobby below the gallery led through to the schoolroom in a lean-to construction at the rear, itself widened in 1933.[143] The chapel was sold in 1989 and converted neatly into two one-bedroom houses by splitting the three tall windows into top and bottom halves – with added stonework, thus avoiding the problems identified above with the Sladesbrook chapel – and creating an extra door at the left hand end.

Providence Baptist interior after closure (Wiltshire Buildings Record)

Providence Baptist reconverted to housing but with signs still of its previous life

4 Chapel People

Nowadays a small minority of people attend church services regularly. This was not the case before the 20th century – the decline in attendance started earlier but was accelerated by the impact of the First World War – and in those circumstances the church inevitably played a much bigger role in nearly everyone's life. So the decision to leave the established church, the Church of England, and join a nonconformist congregation was a major one. What sort of people made such a decision?

In the earliest times, from the late 17th to the mid-18th century, this was a tough choice to make. Even in a town like Bradford, where the support of the clothiers gave some protection, you risked disapproval, ostracism and perhaps even physical violence or being locked up. So anyone becoming a dissenter in those days was probably a person with deeply held and well thought out religious views. Others would likely think the move was just too risky.

The obstacles reduced over time and now other factors could play a part: influence from neighbours and friends, the appeal of a particularly inspiring preacher, or just a desire for change. And it is noticeable how often people worshipped at both Anglican and nonconformist churches, perhaps attending morning service at one and evening service at the other. The town's gentry were probably left untouched by all this and remained loyal to the Church of England; the initial support of the clothiers may also have gradually waned as they were absorbed further into this same class.[144] Amongst most of the townspeople, however, there seems to be no obvious evidence that any one person was more likely to become a nonconformist than any other.

The image we perhaps have associates strong nonconformity with major industrial areas, the Welsh valleys or industrial Lancashire for instance, and it may be that Bradford's many mill workers in the 18th and 19th centuries formed the core of nonconformist congregations; but further research would be needed to demonstrate this. Either way, it is well to bear in mind that by the mid-19th century there were more nonconformists than Anglicans in the town: nonconformists were not some 'other' group; they were most people.

Picking people out to represent this large group would be pointless, but it is possible to identify just a few individuals who had a particular influence on the growth and maintenance of nonconformist life in the town. This chapter continues with notes on just a handful of these.

John Holton, the first of several clothiers in this list, merits his place because he was amongst the first to register a meeting house in the town, taking advantage of Charles II's very temporary 'Declaration of Indulgence' in 1672.[145] His affluence is underlined by the fact that his family was already living in the Chantry at the west end of Church Street at this date and he bought the house in 1676.[146] He was a Presbyterian but it seems he had died before the Grove chapel opened in 1698 so was not associated with it, his children having by that date moved to Bromham.[147] The 1672 registration could possibly have related to another house he owned but it is intriguing to think of this affluent family inviting others into their grand house for Presbyterian worship.

Francis Yerbury (1638-1720) was a member of an even more prominent clothier family and with his youngest son, also Francis, one of the chief protagonists in the creation of the Grove meeting house. He had already in 1692 registered for worship both a barn and his own house[148] and now he helped to set up the new meeting house, a place his family would be associated with for the next hundred years. His elder son John (1678-1728) bought land at Belcombe and started the building works which culminated when John's son, another Francis, commissioned John Wood the Elder of Bath in 1734 to design the extensions which give Belcombe Court so much of its character now.[149]

Zachariah Shrapnel (1662-1723), son of the Henry whose house had been used for Baptist worship since 1672, was a member of another prominent local family, originally coopers but transformed by Zachariah into clothiers, in the process making his fortune.[150] He built the more grand house next door to his father's at 5 St Margaret's Street and owned most of the land on St Margaret's Hill, much of which he thereafter let off in thousand year leases. Although it seems that the family reverted before long to the Church of England, Zachariah at least respected his father's beliefs enough to let the Baptists have the land for their new chapel at a nominal rent.[151] The family is now most famous, perhaps notorious, for Zachariah's 2-greats nephew, Lieutenant General Henry Shrapnel (1761-1842), inventor of the Shrapnel exploding shell.

John Wesley (1703-1791). It might seem presumptuous to claim Wesley for Bradford but he had a profound effect on the development of Methodism in the town. Elected a fellow of Lincoln College, Oxford in 1726, Wesley joined a small group of fellow academics leading a highly disciplined and austere religious life, earning them the nickname 'Methodists'. After various experiences, in 1738 he turned away from this introspective existence and began to preach widely, his evangelical style immediately attracting very large audiences. The Methodists gradually became more and more widely established through the rest of his lifetime and he is said to have travelled around 250,000 miles throughout England, almost all of it on horseback, as he went round the country preaching.

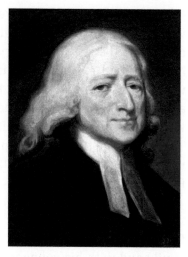

John Wesley, by George Romney (Public domain image)

Bristol was one of his main bases and he came often to Bradford: 6 times in 1739, then a gap of 10 years but at least 26 times more in the rest of his life.[152] The Pippett Street Methodist is thought to have been built largely as a place in which he could preach, although ironically it seems that he developed a dislike for it and preferred to preach outdoors.

Richard Pearce (1715-1794) serves almost as a footnote to Wesley, for it was he who acquired the Maidenhead Inn on Pippett Street (now Market Street, and the Inn in 2024 the Stumble Inn), re-faced it to something like its present appearance in 1755 and built the town's, and the county's, first Methodist chapel on the site of the former malthouse at the back c1756.[153] He remained a stalwart supporter of the Methodist ministers for nearly forty years. As well as being the frequent host for John Wesley and his brother Charles on their visits to Bradford, he nursed another preacher, Thomas Olivers, through a severe attack of smallpox in 1752; in 1757 he offered to stand bail for William Hitchens, a preacher who had been 'pressed for a soldier' and was imprisoned overnight in the bridge lock-up; and in 1790 he hosted Wesley on his last visit to the town. Wesley, by then in his late eighties, had travelled from Frome in a chaise, preaching at Trowbridge on the way; he arrived at 3pm and preached in Bradford at 6. Retiring that night at 9.30pm he was up at 4.30am and on his way to Bristol by 7. Pearce, himself in his mid-70s, must have wondered at the old man's energy.

Joseph Rawling (1792-1866). The story starts with Joseph Rawling's grandfather, also Joseph Rawling, who was a schoolmaster and preacher from Devon.[154] In 1806 he married Mrs Watkins, widow of the former preacher at the Bearfield chapel, and took over as pastor there, though he was not there long, dying in 1813. Joseph the grandson may also have been born in Devon and was a lay preacher from the age of 18. He worked as a printer in Bristol, then Bath, and came to Bradford in 1816 where he set up as a printer and bookseller in Market Street. He moved to bigger premises at what is now called Old Bank House, next door to the Swan Hotel,[155] c1820 and in the early 1840s acquired 29 Market Street, Pearce's former premises in front of the, by then, closed Pippett Street Methodist, a convenient place for his printing equipment. Finally he or his son Charles took over No.28 next door as the town's new post office.

Joseph Rawling
(Bradford on Avon Museum)

This was the foundation of an important town business which lasted until the turn of the century, but Rawling's significance to nonconformity was his other role, at both the Coppice Hill and Bearfield chapels. He was one of the first stewards at Coppice Hill and served it for many years, yet in 1847, the Bearfield chapel without a pastor and apparently not in a good state, he tore himself away from the Methodists and went there as lay pastor. It seems he was motivated both by his grandfather's memory and by pity for the members of the chapel, who were few and not well off. He served at Bearfield until his death, increasing the number of members from seven to 28, having the building renovated in 1849, and installing an organ in the gallery at his own expense in 1850.

Robert Cadby (c1745-1816) is noted in the records as a carpenter but it is evident from his place in the town that he was much more than a humble chippy. He moved to Bradford from Bath in 1785[156] and before long was established as a trustee of the Morgan's Hill Congregational and a justice of the peace[157] as well as owning property on St Margaret's Hill. By about 1805 he was living at 3 Trowbridge Road, a substantial house in a block which he had built;[158] it was later occupied by his son Charles, who followed him in the business, and his daughter Mary.[159] There is much more to be researched about the life of this clearly entrepreneurial man but here we may note that this was someone not from a wealthy background who made an impact in the town, who supported the work of the Congregational chapel over a long period and who may well have been responsible for the design of the 1798 extension to that building. His daughter Mary, who with her brother owned various of the buildings around the chapel, in 1835 gave up some of these to create space for the new schoolroom to be built.[160]

Thomas Ball Silcock (1797-1886), the last in this short list of notables, was another of those whose influence in nonconformist affairs stretched through more than one generation. He was a millwright and joined the Morgan's Hill Congregational in 1818, became Sunday school superintendent and later moved on to other and higher offices there.[161] His first two wives both died but he married a third, Amelia Milsom, in 1853 and they had two sons who followed their parents into the church.

All this would be unexceptional, except that his eldest son was also named Thomas Ball Silcock (1854-1924) and he became a prominent local architect, twice the mayor of Bath and, for one term from 1906 to 1910, the Liberal MP for Wells. All this prominence might have been thought to take him away from his Bradford roots but his list of works[162] shows a marked emphasis on nonconformist chapels and their schoolrooms, including the 1892 alterations to Bearfield recorded above. His major work in Bradford was the Fitzmaurice Grammar School of 1895-6, confident and harmonious on its raised site.

5 Conclusion

The nonconformist chapels assessed in this book are just a few buildings amongst hundreds in Bradford, but their importance far outweighs their number. Through their function as places of worship they have touched the lives of many thousands over the 300 and more years that they have been here. These lives have included often great struggle, hardship and poverty, but also the strength and support of a community of like-minded people as well as times of harmony and relative prosperity. It is surely impossible to view these buildings now without reflecting back on the role they have played over such a long period.

This book has focussed mainly on the history and on the buildings themselves. The rate of chapel survival here is impressive: across Wiltshire only around 30% of the chapels in use in 1900 are still used as such, with the smaller towns averaging about 40%[163] compared to Bradford's 60%. The ones which remain here are in good health and the two which have been converted into houses are in good condition. The main source of regret is the loss of the Coppice Hill Wesleyan Methodist, which is an impressive enough ruin now but how much better if some way could have been found to maintain its splendid interior. Overall, though, the town has a fine collection of chapels which should be valued highly, for their continuing function as centres of religious life and for their major contribution to the shared history of Bradford on Avon.

Notes

General Sources

Most sources are detailed in the individual references but a few of the most prominent are described further here:

Bradford on Avon Museum website, bradfordonavonmuseum.co.uk, has an impressively wide-ranging online collection of historical information and photographs.

British Newspaper Archive – An online collection of newspapers, the source of most newspaper references used here.

Kelly's Directories were issued regularly over a long period from the early 19th century, giving details of individuals, businesses, churches and public bodies in a particular area. Other companies also produced directories but Kelly's were dominant. The University of Leicester has made available a selection online and the Wiltshire and Swindon History Centre at Chippenham has a more comprehensive collection.

Ordnance Survey maps at large scale (25" to the mile) are available online from two main sources, Know Your Place maps at maps.bristol.gov.uk/kyp, and the National Library of Scotland, maps.nls.uk

VCH – Volumes of the Victoria County History for Wiltshire, with volume number. Available online at British-history.ac.uk/vch/wilts.

WBR – Document in the collection of the Wiltshire Buildings Record, available for access at their office in the Wiltshire and Swindon History Centre, Chippenham.

WCH – Wiltshire Community History, an online resource maintained by the Wiltshire and Swindon History Centre at apps.wiltshire.gov.uk/communityhistory

WRS – Volumes of the Wiltshire Record Society, available online at wiltshirerecordsociety.org.uk.

WSA – Documents from the Wiltshire and Swindon Archives at the Wiltshire and Swindon History Centre.

Footnotes

1 There are many sources for the early history of nonconformity. Wiltshire VCH Volume 3, pages 99-149, provides a good introduction for this county

2 *Wiltshire Notes & Queries*, 1893, Volume 2 page 174

3 VCH7 page 32

4 *Ibid*

5 *Ibid*

6 State Papers Domestic Charles II, 1672 Notes of licences, p.205.

7 *Ibid*

8 The evidence for this early date for a meeting house seems weak: the Victoria County History references only a much later map which shows the meeting house.

9 *The Quaker Meeting Houses of Britain*, Volume 2, D M Butler, London, Friends' Historical Society 1999. Again, there seems to be no direct evidence for these claimed dates, although a Quaker meeting house here was registered in 1690 (WRS Volume 40)

10 *The Strict Baptist Chapels of England*, vol 5 Wiltshire and the West, Robert W Oliver, Fauconberg Press 1968

11 *Baptists in Bradford on Avon*, Robert W Oliver, published by the church, 1989.

12 Information on 6-7 St Margaret's Street from Pamela Slocombe, who has surveyed it for the Wiltshire Buildings Record.

13 *The Covenant of the Baptized Church of Christ in Bradford, with a brief history of the Church* (Bradford, 1843), quoted in VCH7 page 32; WRS Volume 40.

14 Family history given on Freshford.com website, accessed 28/3/2024; see also Chapter 4.

15 *Bradford on Avon, a History and Description*, Rev W H Jones, in *Wiltshire Archaeological and Natural History Magazine* 1859 but updated and reprinted by J Beddoe in 1907.

16 WRS Volume 40

17 VCH7 page 33, and for the rest of this paragraph.

18 Independent Meeting to United Church 1740 to 1990, 250 years of Christian Worship in Bradford on Avon, Roger Mawby 1990, quoting church records; WSA3186/2.

19 VCH7 pages 33/4; WSA3186/2.

20 WRS Volume 40

21 WSA3186/2
22 VCH7 page 36
23 Ibid
24 WRS Volume 40
25 VCH7 page 36; Bradford on Avon museum website, accessed 29/3/2024
26 WRS Volume 27. The identity of the second Methodist meeting is not clear: no registration supports the presence of a second meeting place.
27 *The Strict Baptist Chapels of England*, Oliver, op cit.
28 Information on the Quaker meeting house from VCH7 page 33.
29 Description of this chapel from VCH7 page 35.
30 1851 ecclesiastical census returns held in the National Archives
31 Quoted in *Devizes & Wilts Advertiser* 24/11/1881
32 WRS Volume 27
33 VCH7 page 34
34 *The Strict Baptist Chapels of England*, Robert W Oliver, *op cit*
35 VCH7 page37
36 VCH7 page 36
37 WSA2852/14
38 Roger Mawby, op cit.
39 *Wiltshire Times* 2/4/1864
40 VCH7 page 33
41 VCH7 page 35
42 VCH7 page 36.
43 WSA3186/17
44 VCH7 page 33
45 VCH7 page 36; *Salisbury & Winchester Journal* 9/11/1818
46 VCH7 page 36; 1851 ecclesiastical census
47 An Inventory of Nonconformist Chapels and Meeting Houses in South West England, Christopher Stell, Royal Commission on the Historical Monuments of England, 1991
48 But see comment in Chapter 3, below
49 Information in these paragraphs about the Grove and Zion chapels, except where otherwise noted, is from VCH7 page 34
50 The census, which also quoted the capacity of the chapel, was detailed in the *Wiltshire Times* for 19/11/1891.
51 Rev W H Jones, *op cit.*
52 *Baptists in Bradford on Avon*, Oliver op cit.
53 *Wiltshire Independent* 14/9/1843
54 *Wiltshire Times* 2/12/1876
55 *Trowbridge Chronicle* 3/12/1892
56 WRS Volume 40
57 VCH7 page 37
58 *Trowbridge Chronicle* 21/2/1885 and 26/6/1886; *Devizes and Wilts Advertiser* 13/9/1888.
59 Information on the Providence chapel is from VCH7 page 35 unless otherwise stated. It seems that they only bought the property, for £100, in 1864 (WSA2852/14)
60 Ordnance Survey 25" map, 1st edition surveyed 1884/5; Kelly's directory for 1903

61 Information from the website of Bradford on Avon museum, accessed 1/4/2024
62 Information on this chapel from VCH7 page 35 except where otherwise noted.
63 Information on Lady Huntingdon's Connexion is available from numerous sources: a particularly useful one is *Methodism*, Rupert E Davies, Penguin, 1963.
64 *Wiltshire Independent* 12/9/1844
65 Although it seems it was never made over legally to the Congregational Union, an omission which meant they could not secure funding from the English Congregational Chapel Building Society when they wished to make improvements in 1914 (WSA4335/3)
66 For example, Wiltshire *Times* 10/6/1933
67 *The Quakers of Melksham*, Harold Fassnidge, Bradford on Avon Friends 1992
68 WSA 1273/10
69 *Wiltshire Independent* 9/11/1837.
70 *Wiltshire Independent* 8/3/1838.
71 Roger Mawby, op cit.
72 1851 ecclesiastical census
73 *The Strict Baptist Chapels of England*, Oliver, op cit.
74 VCH7 page 35
75 *Wiltshire Times* 20/6/2015 records the 135th anniversary of its foundation.
76 For example, *Trowbridge Chronicle* 23/9/1882 and *Devizes & Wiltshire Gazette* 18/9/1890.
77 *Trowbridge Chronicle* 5/8/1882; *Devizes & Wiltshire Gazette* 18/9/1890; *Warminster & Westbury Journal* 20/9/1890; WSA4186/1A/93
78 Information supplied by Dr Tim Grass, researcher into this sect.
79 *Devizes & Wiltshire Gazette* 26/1/1854
80 For example, *Wiltshire Times* 14/10/1876
81 *Trowbridge Chronicle*, 29/11/1897
82 WSA1273/10; Devizes & Wilts Advertiser, 4/10/1894
83 Website of Bradford on Avon Quakers, accessed 3/4/2024; WSA2269/26
84 Website of Bradford on Avon museum, accessed 4/4/2024
85 Information on the period from 1939 onwards supplied by the church.
86 Information on the last years of the Coppice Hill Wesleyan from the website of Bradford on Avon museum, accessed 3/4/2024
87 WSA1594/8
88 *Wiltshire Times* 16/9/1933; WSA2852/14
89 WSA2852/14; WBR B7409
90 Information about the 20th century history of the Old Baptist from Baptists in Bradford on Avon, Oliver, op cit.
91 See for example *Wiltshire Times* 21/8/1937
92 WBR B4130; WSA3186/30
93 For example *Salisbury and Winchester Journal* 13/9/1819
94 *Wiltshire Times* 10/9/1881 records baptisms still in the river, with a crowd of 'between 2000 and 3000 persons,' but by 1899 baptisms were being carried

out in the church (*Wiltshire Times* 26/8/1899). Julian Orbach, however, in his notes for the new *Buildings of England* for Wiltshire, suggests the tank was inserted in 1860.

95 *The Buildings of England, Wiltshire*, Julian Orbach, Nikolaus Pevsner and Bridget Cherry, Yale University Press 2021

96 Julian Orbach, index of Wiltshire architects

97 Architects and Buildings Craftsmen with work in Wiltshire, Part 2, Pamela M Slocombe, Wiltshire Buildings Record 2006.

98 VCH7 page 32; Andrew's and Dury's map of Wiltshire 1773 shows an approximate location.

99 VCH7 page 33

100 D M Butler, op cit.

101 VCH7 page 33

102 VCH7 page 33

103 D M Butler, op cit.

104 D M Butler, op cit.

105 WSA854/37

106 *Wiltshire Times* 'March of Time' article 26/9/1980.

107 D M Butler, *op cit.*

108 *The Year of the Map – Portrait of a Wiltshire town in 1841*, Gee Langdon, Compton Russell 1976

109 *Wiltshire Times* 2/12/1876

110 WSA2544/13

111 *Trowbridge Chronicle* 28/11/1876

112 WSA2544/13

113 WSA2544/13; *Wiltshire Times* 2/12/1876

114 *Trowbridge Chronicle* 26/11/1892

115 *Trowbridge Chronicle* 28/11/1876

116 Historic England listing

117 *Baptists in Bradford on Avon*, Robert W Oliver, published by the church, reprinted 2005.

118 A photograph in the possession of Bradford on Avon Museum shows this, as do old Ordnance Survey maps.

119 Roger Mawby, op cit

120 This account of the chapel's building history is derived from Roger Mawby, op cit; WSA3186/2; Julian Orbach, notes for the new Wiltshire *Buildings of England*; and personal observation.

121 The design perhaps by Robert Cadby (see chapter introduction)

122 Roger Mawby, op cit, suggests there may have been two doors in the front wall at this date but a late 18th century plan (WSA3186/27) shows only one.

123 Roger Mawby, op cit.

124 WSA1418/9

125 WBR B1034

126 WCH

127 WBR B1034

128 WSA3909/1

129 WSA1418/9

130 WCH

131 Personal communication with the church secretary.

132 Julian Orbach, notes to the new Wiltshire *Buildings of England*

133 WSA453/3

134 WSA453/3

135 Julian Orbach, Wiltshire architects list, available online in 2024

136 1851 religious census

137 The exact construction date has not been identified but it was certainly in place by 1863 (*Wiltshire Times* 11/4/1863)

138 The house was gone by the end of the 19th century (Ordnance Survey 1885 and 1899 revisions)

139 *Devizes and Wilts Advertiser* 13/9/1888

140 WCH

141 Historic England listing

142 Description of interior from 1988 survey in WBR B7409.

143 WSA2852/14

144 The Shrapnels are one example – see below – but one of the Yerburys was still worshipping at the Grove chapel in the 1790s and Joseph Rawling commented that in the early 19th century 'the rich and influential in Bradford and vicinity did not consider themselves out of place or lowering their position to attend a Wesleyan ministry.' (*Bradford on Avon Past & Present*, Harold Fassnidge, revised edition, Ex Libris Press 2007)

145 VCH7 page 32

146 Rev W H Jones, *op cit.*

147 Jones, op cit

148 WRS Volume 40

149 Bradford on Avon museum website, accessed 13/5/2024

150 Except where otherwise noted, information about the Shrapnels is derived from various records gathered together on the freshford.com website, accessed 13/5/2024.

151 VCH7 page 34

152 Fassnidge, op cit

153 Description of Pearce is mostly from VCH7 page 36

154 Information in this section from VCH7 and Fassnidge, *op cit*, except where otherwise noted

155 Information from Bradford on Avon museum

156 Julian Orbach, notes in preparation for the new *Buildings of England*, Wiltshire

157 Langdon, *op cit*; Roger Mawby, op cit

158 Information from Bradford on Avon museum

159 1851 census returns

160 Roger Mawby, op cit

161 Roger Mawby, op cit for information in this section except where otherwise noted.

162 Julian Orbach, Wiltshire architects list

163 *Wiltshire Nonconformist Chapels and Meeting Houses*, James Holden, Wiltshire Buildings Record 2022.

More publications from Bradford-on-Avon Museum

- **The Christopher Pharmacy** by Ivor Slocombe & Roger Clark
  A5; 14 pages; full colour; Price £2.00
- **Lost Pubs of Bradford on Avon: A Walker's Guide** by Roger Clark;
  A5; 12 pages; full colour; Price £2.50
- **Abbey Mill** by David Gazard
  A5; 16 pages; full colour; Price £3.00
- **Bradford-on-Avon Printers and Town Directories**
  by Roger Jones; A5; 28 pages; Price £2.50
- **The Saxon Church** by David A. Hinton
  A5; 24 pages; full colour; Price £4.00
- **The Hall, Bradford-on-Avon** by Pamela M. Slocombe
  Large format; 44 pages; full colour; Price £4.00
- **The Bridges of Bradford-on-Avon** by Ivor Slocombe
  A5; 28 pages; full colour; Price £4.00
- **The Woollen Industry at Bradford-on-Avon** by Kenneth Rogers
  A5; 24 pages; full colour; Price £3.00
- **Geology, Landscape and Building Stone around Bradford-on-Avon**
  by Isobel Geddes; A5; 28 pages; Price £3.00
- **The Buildings of Barton Farm, Bradford-on-Avon** by Pamela M. Slocombe
  and Ivor Slocombe; Large format; 48 pages; full colour; Price £4.00
- **The Iron Duke: The machine that founded Bradford-on-Avon's rubber industry**
  by Roger Clark. 8 pages; full colour; Price £1.00
- **Bradford Leigh Fair: 200 Years of Trade, Revelry, Wickedness and Vice**
  by Robert Arkell. A5; 44 pages; Price £4.00
- **Rubber Town** by Dan Farrell
  Large format;134 pages with many illustrations; £10.00
- **Whooosh!: Billy and Bella meet the Memory Keeper**
  by Gill Winfield and illustrated by Mike Dickinson; 54 pages; full colour;
  Price £5.00
- **Bradford-on-Avon: The 1841 Map** Introduction by Ivor Slocombe
  Large format; 32 large format pages; Price £5.00
- **Improving Life in nineteenth century Bradford-on-Avon**
  by Ivor Slocombe. A5; 48 pages; full colour; £5.00

Bradford-on-Avon Museum monographs ~

- **Anglo-Saxon Bradford-on-Avon** by Martin Whittock and Hannah Whittock
  A5; 28 pages; Price £3.00
- **Bradford-on-Avon: the Medieval Town** by Ivor & Pamela Slocombe
  A5; 32 Pages; Price £3.00
- **Bradford-on-Avon 1500-1700** by Ivor and Pamela Slocombe
  Large format; 62 pages; full colour; Price£7.50
- **Budbury from hillfort to houses** by Pamela Slocombe and Roy Canham
  Large format; 80 pages; full colour; Price £7.50
- **Bradford-on-Avon Probate Inventories 1550–1700** by Ivor Slocombe
  138 pages; Price £6.00
- **A History of Rowley-Wittenham: Deserted Medieval Village
  and Lost Parish** by Robert Arkell; 96 pages; full colour; Price £8.00
- **A Vanished World** by Margaret Dobson
  100 pages; full colour; Price £10.00

Copies of any of these titles are available from Bradford on Avon Museum
www.bradfordonavonmuseum.co.uk